FROM THE NEW YORK TIMES BEST-SELLING AUTHOR

SOCIAL POETRY

I0484268

Boosting engagement and encouraging conversation by using inspirational, educational and entertaining photoquotes

JOEL COMM

Social Poetry: Boosting Engagement and Encouraging Conversation by Using Inspirational, Educational and Entertaining Photoquotes

Welcome to Social Poetry

A picture says a thousand words, the adage is oft-repeated. It's true that pictures frequently say more than what can be contained by the English language. That's one reason social media is rife with photographs and images. We like to SEE.

So what happens when you add words to pictures? Something new. Words can highlight a facet of the image, convey a new thought or make a funny picture even funnier. Whether the words are designed to instruct, inspire or entertain, when combined with a picture, something memorable can be created.

In the social media world, that something memorable is often liked, commented on, or shared by the community. I've been a big fan of posting photos since I started using social media in 2007. However, I'm not a Photoshop expert by any stretch. In fact, I'm as amateur as they get.

But with the introduction of some great apps, I now find myself frequently sharing my thoughts and feelings with my followers by posting photos with text imposed upon them. In fact, the latest apps are so powerful that the resulting images look more professional than anything I could ever hope to create with Photoshop.

As it turns out, people enjoy the photos that I post. At least it seems they do as the photos receive plenty of engagement. It was a Friday at Ken McArthur's Impact Event in Denver, Colorado in Fall 2014.

I was to speak on Saturday, but I had just gotten home after a 2-week run of events and speaking engagements in multiple cities. I hadn't had an opportunity to put together a presentation for the event attendees and I wasn't certain what direction I wanted to go.

I was sitting at lunch with several of the attendees when one of them asked me what I was going to speak on. I honestly replied that I didn't know, and I asked those at the table what they would like to hear from me. One of the attendees mentioned that she enjoyed the photoquotes that I posted on social media and asked whether I could share some of them. I puzzled on it for a couple minutes and then it clicked in my mind.

There is a story behind each and every photoquote I post. Sometimes it is something I want to say about business. Other times it's something I want to say about life. And then there are the time when I am just being silly. And while the photoquotes speak for themselves, I thought it would be interesting to present a collection of them and spend a minute or two elaborating on what I said and what I wanted people to understand.

I immediately got to work on creating a new presentation centered around these photoquotes and the story behind them. I was excited to share new material with this audience! The presentation received fantastic accolades. And afterwards several of the attendees suggested that I take the material and turn it into a book.

While formatted for digital reading, you may be holding a physical copy right now. Either way, you may consider this is a coffee-table book of sorts. Designed to pick up and casually read when you just want a quick thought or to go all the way through in one short sitting, the more-than-fifty photoquotes, and the stories behind them, contained within this book will instruct, inspire and entertain you.

All the photoquotes within were selected based on the interaction and engagement they received. I figure if my social media friends enjoyed them, you may as well. Consider them my gift to you. It's my hope that you enjoy my social poetry, and that you are encouraged to create some of your own.

Now that's enough words. Let's allow the pictures to do the talking.

EVERYONE HAS
a story.
-joel comm

One day I took a picture of collection of books I had written, along with the foreign translations. These were my stories. But I quickly observed that each and every one of us has valuable stories to tell. It's only fitting that I start this book with this photoquote, because ultimately it's my hope that these images inspire you to tell your story.

Nobody likes to be judged. One day someone posted a judgmental thought towards me on my Facebook page. I'm a big believer in allowing others to be who they are within needing to make sense of it. I don't feel a need to explain myself or my choices to others, so I assume others have the same freedom.

When you think about the water-cooler at the office, yes, it's there for a drink. But what's it really there for? Socializing. And what are people talking about when they pull away from their desk and go to that water-cooler and see other people there? Everything and anything. That's precisely what social media is like. It's a place where people can talk about everything and anything. Just because we are behind our computers and can't see other people doesn't mean they don't exist. They share similar hopes, dreams, fears, feelings, wishes, hurts and experiences.

"People who don't grow and change can't relate to people who do"
-Joel Comm

JoelComm
.com

This is one of the ones that I posted after I came through a period of personal growth myself. Some of you may not know that I took a Sabbatical for a couple of years back in 2011 and 2012. I took almost two years off. I sold off my large properties, let go of my entire team of 38 people over the period of year and a half. It was a transformative period for me to work on myself physically, emotionally and spiritually. And it takes someone who has had a transformative experience to understand true growth and change.

"Your best days are before you."

JOELComm.com

Optimism is contagious. But I don't believe it's just feel-good thinking. All the experiences we've had in our life, both the positive and the negative, help shape us into who we are today. If we learn and grow from all our experiences, we build upon our lives. That means who we have become is stronger, smarter and wiser than who we were. How can you not be optimistic that the best is yet to come?!

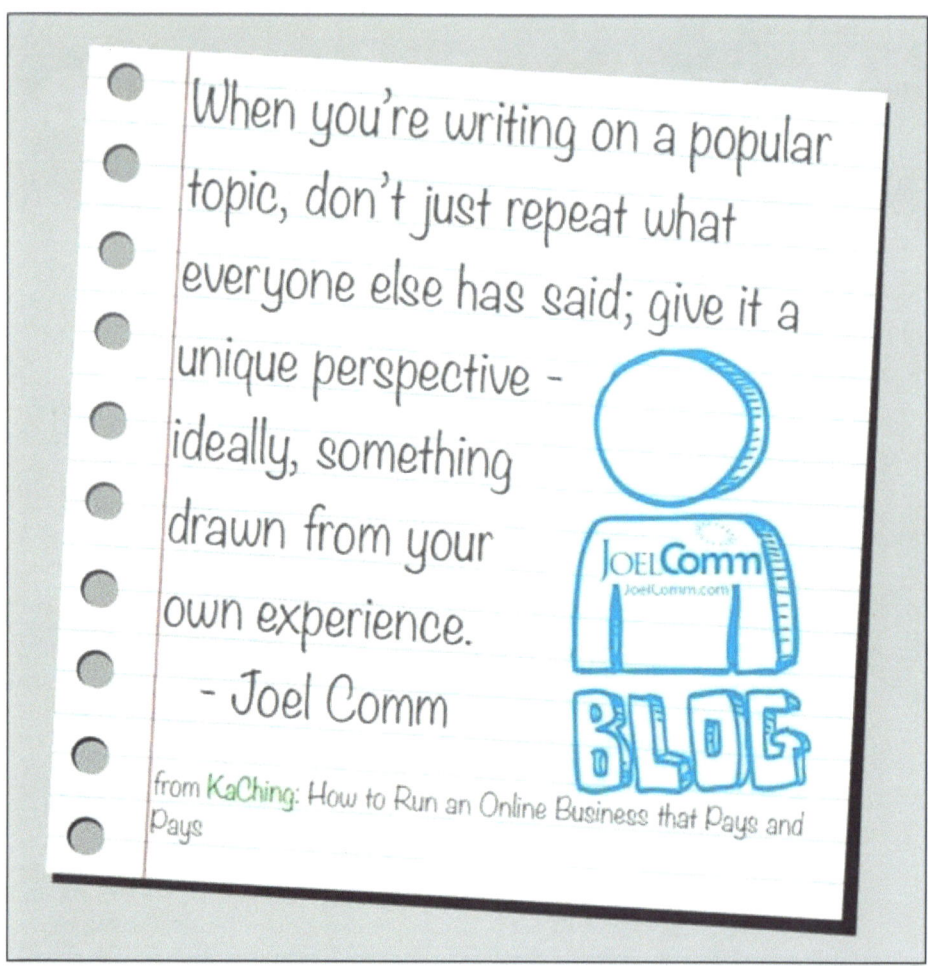

When you're writing on a popular topic, don't just repeat what everyone else has said; give it a unique perspective - ideally, something drawn from your own experience.

- Joel Comm

from KaChing: How to Run an Online Business that Pays and Pays

It seems like there is a new fitness, nutrition and parenting guru every year or so. Why is that? Don't we have enough books on these topics already? The truth is that everyone brings a uniqueness to the conversation, and everything has not yet been said... because you haven't said your part! It's important to bring your unique perspective to the conversation. It may be just the thing that someone needs to hear.

Sometimes the conversation in social media can seem like a whole lot of nonsense and blabber. So instead of saying something profound, I decided to just tell it like it is. Admit it, we all feel this way from time to time.

I often believe others are much better subject matter for a photoquote than me. At the conference mentioned in my introduction, I took this photo of Ken McArthur, who I dubbed "the nicest guy in Internet marketing". It was such a great picture of Ken! And that day I heard him say this in passing conversation. I knew I had to Wordswag it!

Yesterday was a good day, but today is going to be even better!
- Joel Comm

Can you handle some more optimism? I don't think we can get enough. If our perspective is in line when we get up each morning, we'll recognize that life is a gift. I'm grateful that I get to do what I do with people that I like. Life is good, so why not anticipate that today is going to be a fantastic day!

I'M NOT GETTING A THING DONE TODAY... And that's OKAY!

— Joel Comm —

It's really easy to fill our life with busyness and forget to just chill out on occasion. It was a Monday and I had plenty I needed to get done. But I just wasn't feeling it. So I decided to take the day off and I proudly stated that I was being unproductive, at least as far as work was concerned. Knowing when you need time to just enjoy your life can be highly productive for your mental, physical and spiritual health.

We are complicated beings. No one likes being defined by our individual characteristics, whether they are based on our physical appearance, personality, likes or dislikes, or any other single attribute. However, our culture is known for labeling people. "Oh, he's a Republican", or "She's religious". There is so much more to us than any one characteristic. I think it provides us with a sense of understanding if we can slap a label on someone, but the truth is that we don't like it when someone does it to us. See people as deep wells of complex beauty and you won't be tempted to label them so quickly.

The "@" symbol has become the "Hey you!" of social networking.

-Joel Comm

JoelComm
JoelComm.com

The Hashtag and the "@" symbol have become a ubiquitous part of our culture. When we use the "@" symbol, it's like tapping someone on the shoulder and saying "Hey, I'm talking to you. Pay attention!"

I don't like when anyone tells me what to do. I'm a grown man and I can figure out for myself what I want to do. When someone says "You should be on Google Plus" or "You should try this diet", I instinctively want to push back. Our individual freedom and liberty are among the greatest gifts we have. Don't let anyone "should" on you. That said, I always welcome opinions when they are solicited.

"It is the rule-breakers who become the world-changers"

JOEL Comm
JoelComm.com

You want to change the world? You've got to be willing to do things differently. That means you may need to break the rules. I'm not suggesting you break the law, but even civil disobedience can be an ethical agent for change. Don't be afraid to take risks and stand out if you want to make an impact.

Does this one really need any commentary? ;-)

Revolutions, not Resolutions.

2014.

JOEL**Comm**
JoelComm.com

When New Year's comes around and people start talking about resolutions, I always bristle just a little bit. Why wait for the new year to make a change in your life? Resolutions usually don't work because while we may desire to exercise more, quit smoking or make some other significant change, we often want something else more. You can make a change any day of your life. It requires a revolution in your thinking and behavior, nothing more. As that great little muppet sage Yoda once said, "There is no try, only do" (It helps if you can imagine me using my Yoda voice.)

TODAY BECKONS YOU TO EXPLORE AND DISCOVER SOMETHING NEW. WHAT ARE YOU WAITING FOR? -JOEL COMM

I woke up one morning and wasn't sure what I was going to do with my day when I came across this picture. I thought, "Wow, what an adventure. I want to go wherever that is!" Today stands before you. Why not look at each day, really look at each day as an adventure? I'm not saying you have to jump out of an airplane or place yourself in some other kind of danger, but living today... in the moment, is a secret to success.

"Surround yourself with smart people doing cool things."

JoelComm.com

No man is an island. We need each other. I attribute a great deal of my success to the people who I have surrounded myself with. It's true that a rising tide lifts all boats and I have been privileged to be around smart people that are into doing stuff that I think is cool. It's one of the reasons I show up at conferences whether I'm speaking or not. You never know who you are going to meet and what wonderful thing may result from the new relationships you can form.

In the entire history of the world, you are the only you. I think that's pretty dang cool.

Joel Comm

We all strive to be significant, to matter. The thing is, when we are living out our lives following our God-given passions, talents, skills, abilities and personality, we don't have to try hard. We are who we are, and there has never been (nor will ever be) anyone like you. I find that remarkable. YOU are remarkable!

"Someone who uses social media successfully doesn't just create content; he or she creates conversations."
-from Twitter Power 2.0: How to Dominate Your Market One Tweet at a Time

Content is king. Content is KaChing. But your content should do more than provide something for people to read. It should stimulate thought, conversation and action. True social media experts do this without thinking. It's natural.

> # WHEN YOU ASK SOMEONE SO, WHAT DO YOU DO?
> ---
> ## DON'T WAIT FOR THEM
> # TO FINISH SO
> ### YOU CAN TALK ABOUT YOURSELF.
> # STOP AND LISTEN
> # TO THEIR RESPONSE.
> ### IF THEY CARE ABOUT WHAT THEY DO,
> ---
> ## THEIR ANSWER IS
> ## A WINDOW TO THE SOUL.
> ## -JOEL COMM

The question "So, what do you do?" is not just an invitation to learn what someone does vocationally. Assuming the other person is passionate about what they do means their answer is going to be important. Listen carefully and you may learn far more than how they spend their day. They may share a piece of themselves with you.

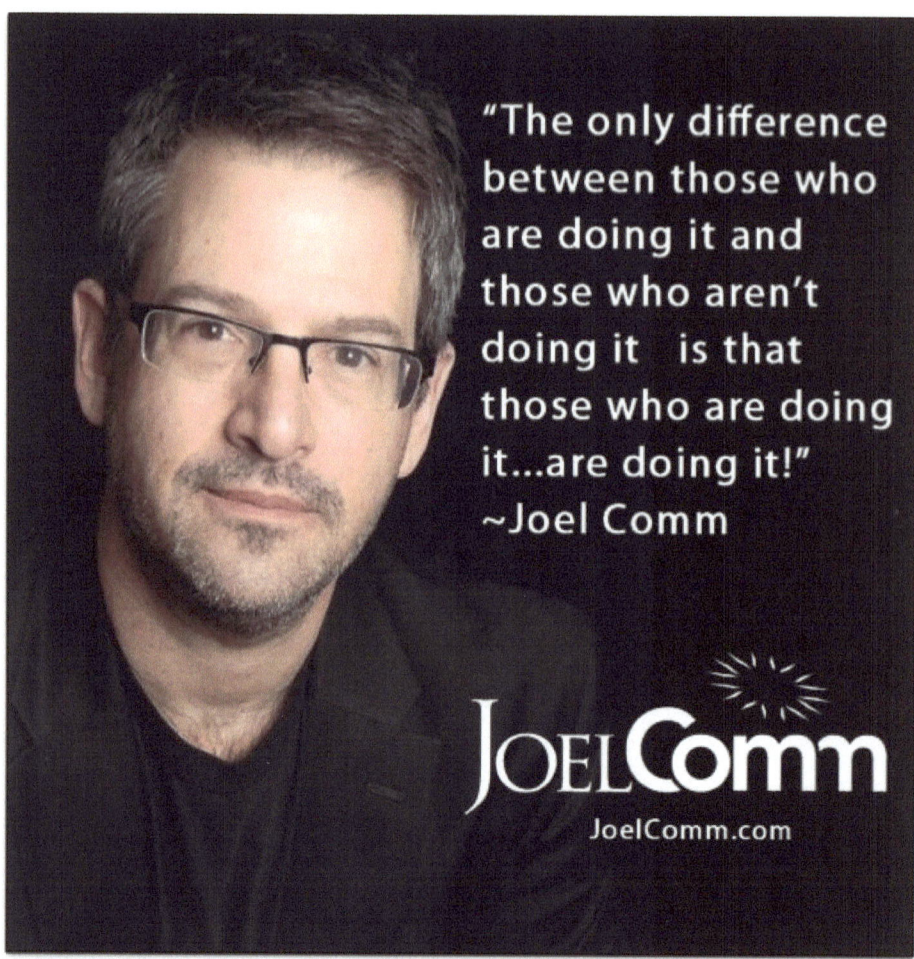

"The only difference between those who are doing it and those who aren't doing it is that those who are doing it...are doing it!"
~Joel Comm

This one may sound stupid, but I think it's profoundly stupid.

Nike had it right. Just do it. It's not complicated.

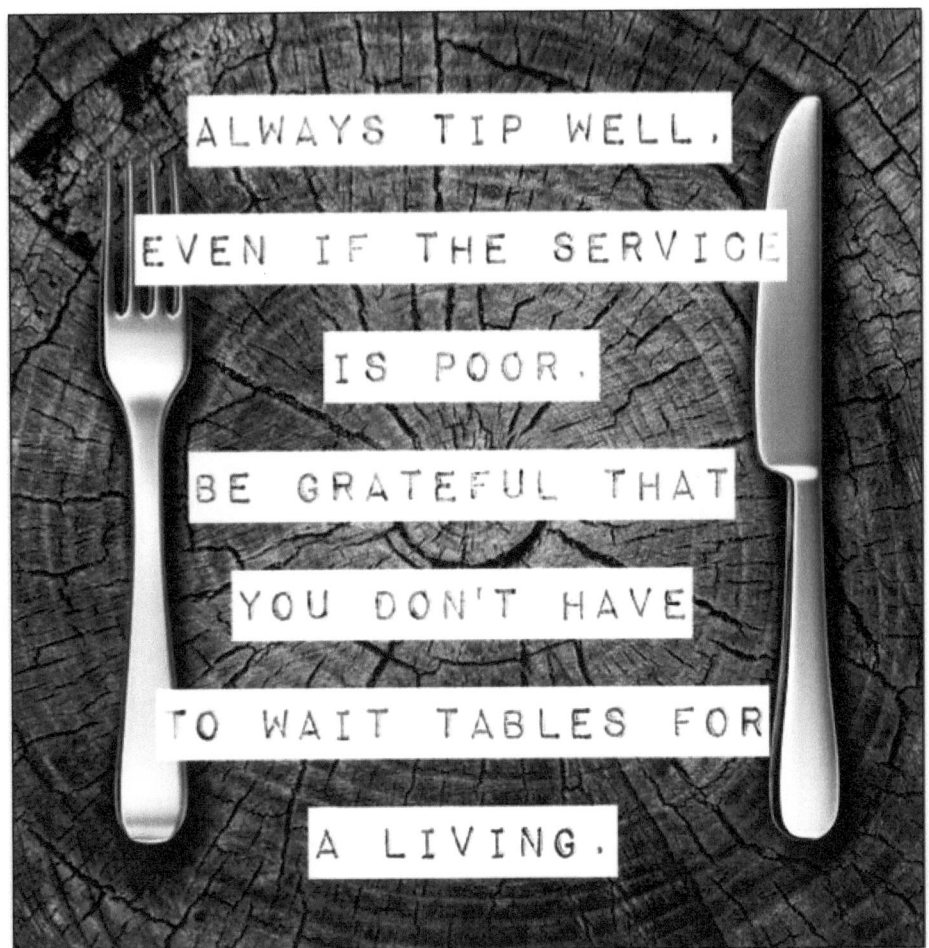

ALWAYS TIP WELL,
EVEN IF THE SERVICE
IS POOR.
BE GRATEFUL THAT
YOU DON'T HAVE
TO WAIT TABLES FOR
A LIVING.

I know people who tip their server purely based on performance. I like to tip 20% as standard, regardless of the service I receive. I am grateful that I get to do what I do, and I figure that if I receive poor service it's often because my server is not happy being a server. I have great respect for those who choose to serve, and especially those who take pride in their work. But I can relate to the frustration of doing a job that I don't really want to do. These people need kind people in their lives, especially if they are having a bad day.

"Don't just tell us what you're doing; tell us what you think about what you're doing."

Joel Comm

from *Twitter Power*

It's one thing to share what you are doing on social media, but what most people are looking for is a human connection. It's not only appropriate to share your thoughts and feelings about what you are doing, it helps connect you with your followers and fans.

IF THE PRESIDENT OF THE UNITED STATES CAN'T GET MORE THAN 50% OF THE POPULATION TO LIKE HIM,

---

WHY SHOULD YOU EXPECT EVERYONE TO LIKE YOU? JUST BE YOU!

-JOEL COMM

We all want to be liked by others. But no matter how hard you try, you are not going to win over everyone. If the leader of the free world has a hard time winning over 50% of the population, I think it's alright that our approval ratings may not be 100%. Besides, we're not designed to be people-pleasers.

I believe that everyone is created by God with unique passions, talents, skills, abilities, personality and presence. You are unique and here for a reason!

JOEL Comm
JoelComm.com

We aren't perfect, but we are wonderfully designed with purpose, value and significance. When you accept this truth, you are free to be who you are and bring value to the world around you.

Sometimes social media can become contentious, especially during political season. I contend that we have much more in common than not. If you are overwhelmed at the conversation taking place, shut off your computer and mobile devices to go view a sunset. That will put things in perspective.

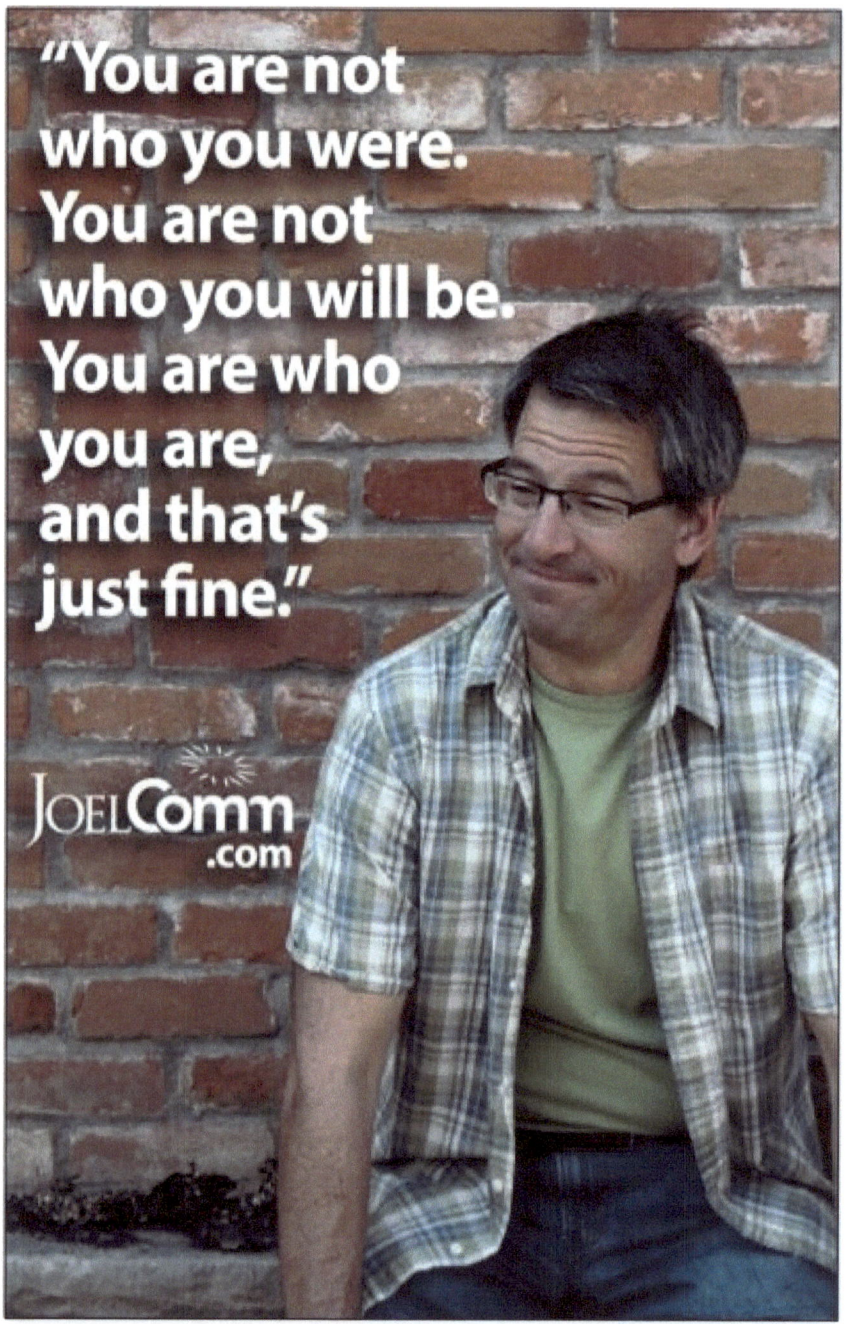

"You are not who you were. You are not who you will be. You are who you are, and that's just fine."

JoelComm
.com

There are time we think we should be further along in our journey than where we are. But I believe we are exactly where we need to be. There's great freedom in acceptance. We don't have to strive to be anywhere else than here and now. Acceptance.

"Once you know your stuff, it's not what you know, it's WHO you know."

JOELComm
JoelComm.com

I assume that everyone is an expert at something. There's a reason you do what you do, and you are likely good at it. We can always seek to learn more about our area of interest, becoming even better at what we do. But ultimately, once you know more than others, you are qualified to help them. At this point, the people you know (and who know you) become more essential to getting your message out. It's really not what you know, but who you know.

"MOO"
-THE COW

I have a confession to make. I can be extremely silly. And I don't plan on stopping any time soon. With so many people sharing inspirational and educational photoquotes, I saw this photo of a cow and remembered the Fisher-Price barnyard sound toy I had when I was child. What does the cow say in the social media age? The same thing she's always said!

I am, and have always been a dreamer. This quote from my favorite childhood film sums up a core part of my philosophy towards business and life.

I DON'T BELIEVE IN LUCK. I BELIEVE IN DESTINY.
– JOEL COMM

I am not a believer in chance or in luck. I don't think it exists. I think we make it up to try to give words to what we think is random happenstance. I don't believe that anybody is here right now at this very moment by accident. I believe in destiny.

OPPORTUNITY MAKERS SPUR US TO USE OUR BEST TALENTS TOGETHER TO CREATE SOMETHING GREATER
-KARE ANDERSON

#TEDatIBM

I recently saw my friend Kare Anderson give a TEDx talk in San Francisco. She said something during her presentation that I had to turn into a photoquote. When we are an opportunity maker, we seek to create something new, special and dynamic with others. The effectiveness is multiplied when smart people with good hearts come together to do something cool.

Sometimes I feel like the energizer bunny. I just keep going and going. But even though I'm busy, I can stop and smell the roses. There were no roses near this wall, but I love how relaxed I am in this photo. If there aren't roses around, a wall will do for chilling and reflecting.

More silliness. This one taken during a recent photo shoot was begging for something less profound.

If you need to sum up the whole of social media, I suppose a cat riding bacon through space could do just the trick.

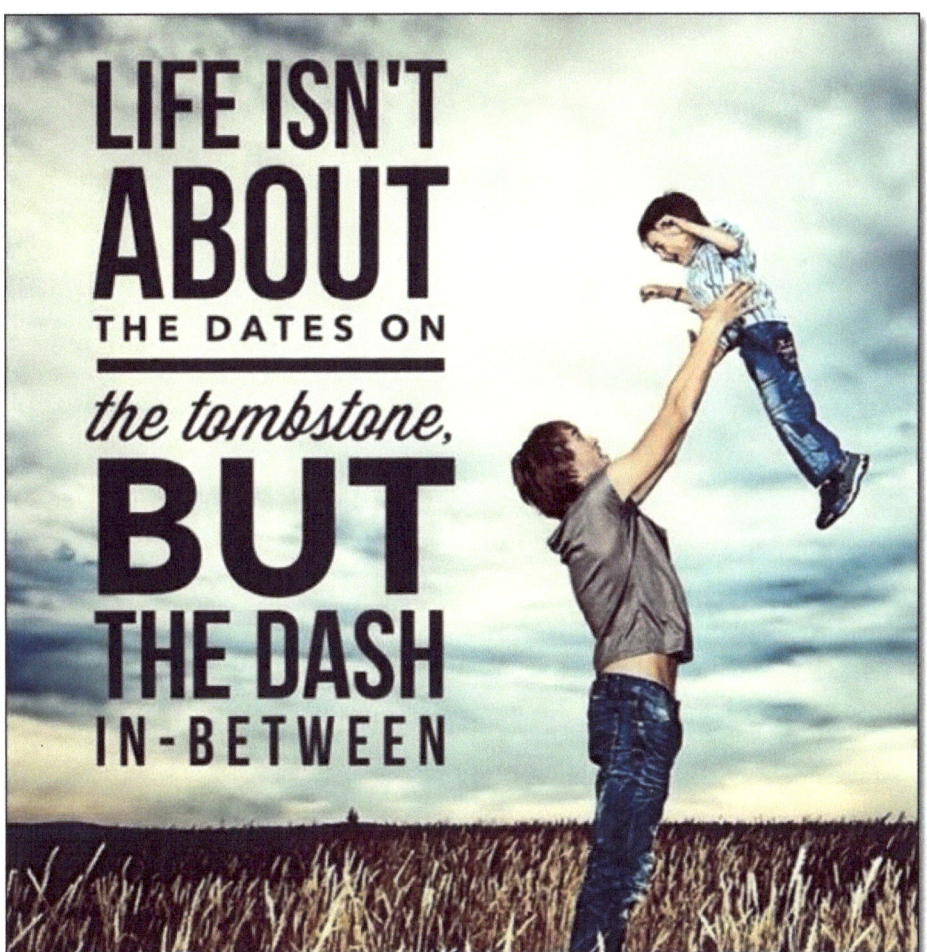

I didn't come up with this quote, but as I reflected on a friend who publicly announced and mourned the loss of his father via Facebook, I thought this photo of a father and son seizing the moment was a great reminder to live the life we have while we still have it.

YOU'RE
NEVER TOO OLD
FOR SOME POOH
-JOEL COMM

If you tell me to grow up, I'm likely respond with a wholehearted "No!" I grew up loving all things Disney, and I still enjoy going to the theme parks when in Orlando or Los Angeles. I took this gangsta' photo with Pooh and had to chuckle at the play on words that came forth.

Your life is your own. No one else can live it for you.

On May 5th, 2014, I turned fifty-years old. I thought it would be a big deal. It wasn't. I feel better at fifty than I did at forty! I posted this on May 6th. I thought it was funny. You can laugh now.

I've already discussed the importance of surrounding yourself with smart people doing cool things, but I wanted to reinforce the idea in this photo of myself with some wonderful friends. (left to right: me, Brian Moran, Bryan Kramer, Adam Helweh, Tim Washer). By showing up a Cisco Live 2014 in San Francisco, I had the opportunity to hang out with these kind and brilliant people. Here we are in the San Francisco Giants away-team dugout during a special VIP concert with Imagine Dragons and Lenny Kravitz. The relationships you form are the most valuable assets you have.

YOUR WEBCAM IS ON. I SEE WHAT YOU ARE DOING. STOP IT.

With all the talk regarding privacy and the NSA snooping on people, I thought I'd get a little creepy with this one. Here I am staring at you, as though I'm voyeuristically watching you through your webcam. There were probably a few people I made uncomfortable with this one. Mission accomplished.

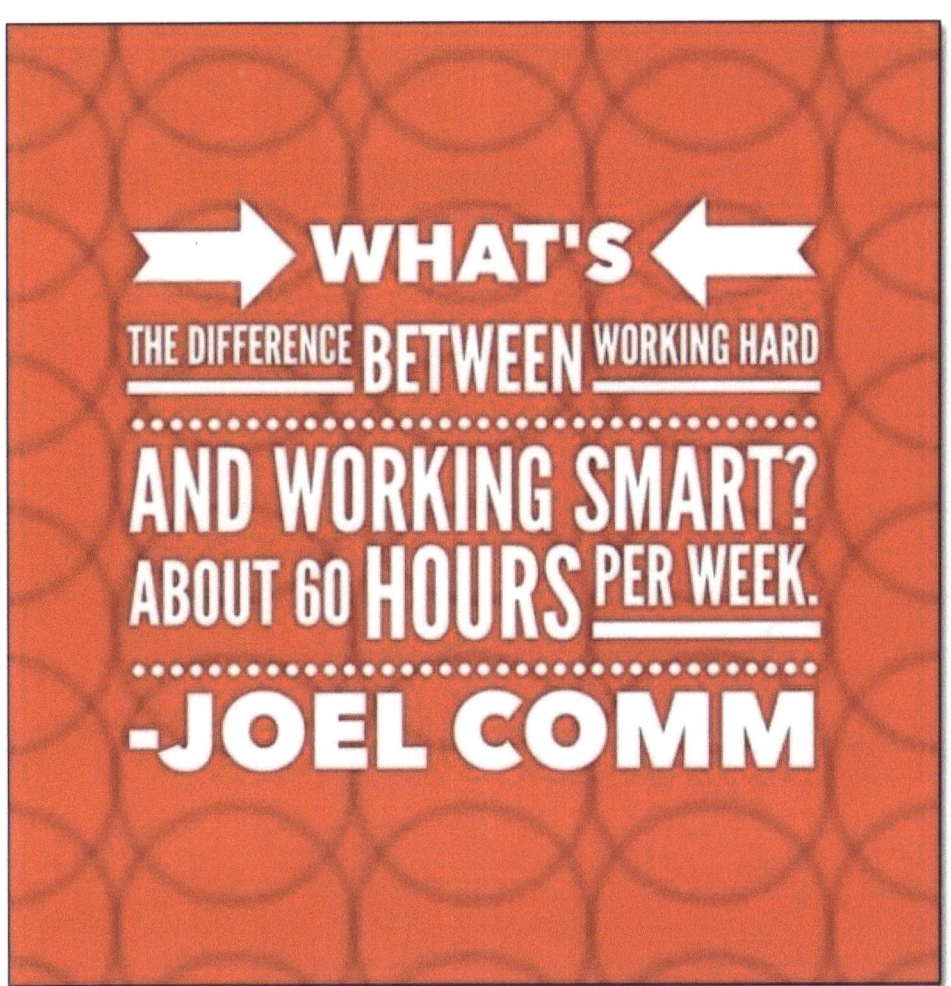

WHAT'S THE DIFFERENCE BETWEEN WORKING HARD AND WORKING SMART? ABOUT 60 HOURS PER WEEK. -JOEL COMM

There's clearly a time and season for hard work. But once you have honed your craft, I believe working smart becomes more important than working hard. I would rather find opportunity at its tipping point than work to create new opportunity. When I look at my biggest successes, I see a pattern. The things that were the turning points were actually the things that didn't take a lot of time and didn't require a lot of effort. A well-timed email; responding to a phone call; the right joint venture partner: none of these took any great effort.

So many businesses are all about the business. They take themselves SO seriously. That's fine for them, but not me. If I'm not having fun then I'm probably not going to succeed at the task. I adopted the flying monkey as my company mascot around 2007. Since that time, I have sent dozens of them in the mail to my peers and associates. I often fling one into the audience from the stage. And I've been known to make silly videos featuring the flying monkey. People remember this about me. And that's the point.

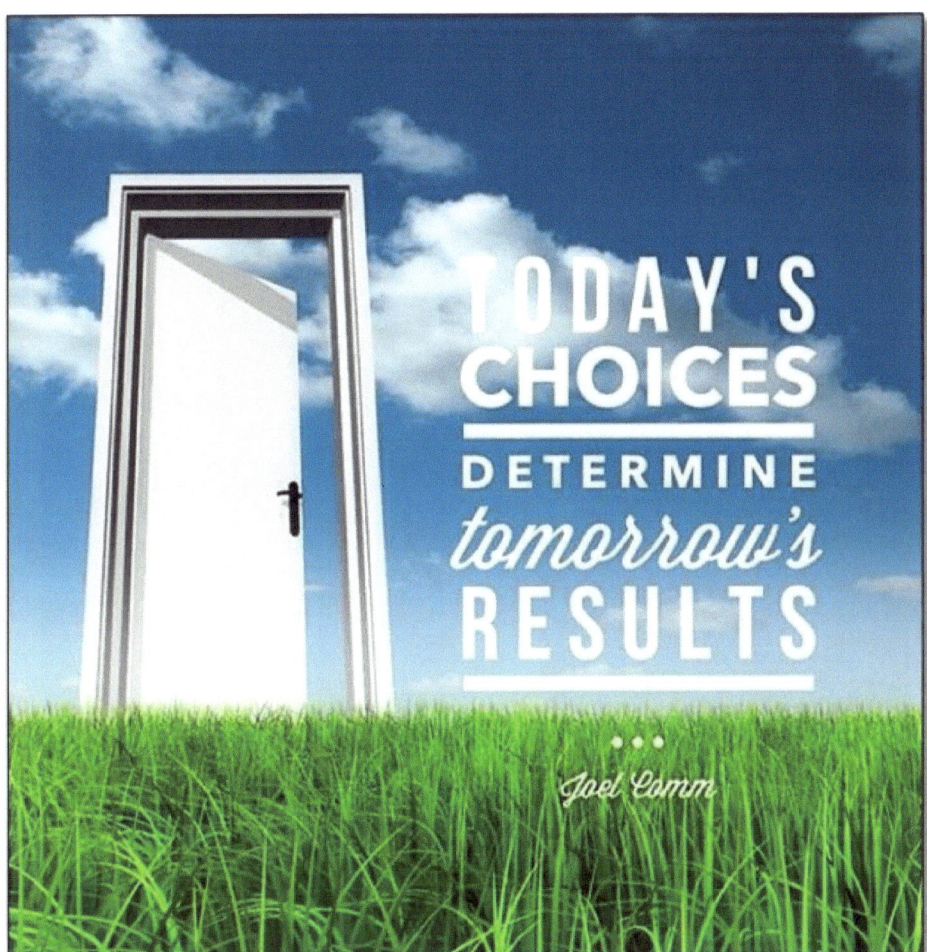

What choices do we make today? The choices that we make today are going to determine the results tomorrow. It's all about choices. Whenever I hear people blaming somebody else for what's happening in their life, especially the negative things, I wonder how many of those consequences can be traced back to poor choices.

I KNOW IT IS WET AND THE SUN IS NOT SUNNY, BUT WE CAN HAVE LOTS OF GOOD FUN THAT IS FUNNY. -DR. SEUSS

This was another silly day. Dr. Seuss was a part of my life and then the lives of my children who I read his books to. It just so happens that I own a "Cat in the Hat" hat and found this to be an appropriate nod to playfulness.

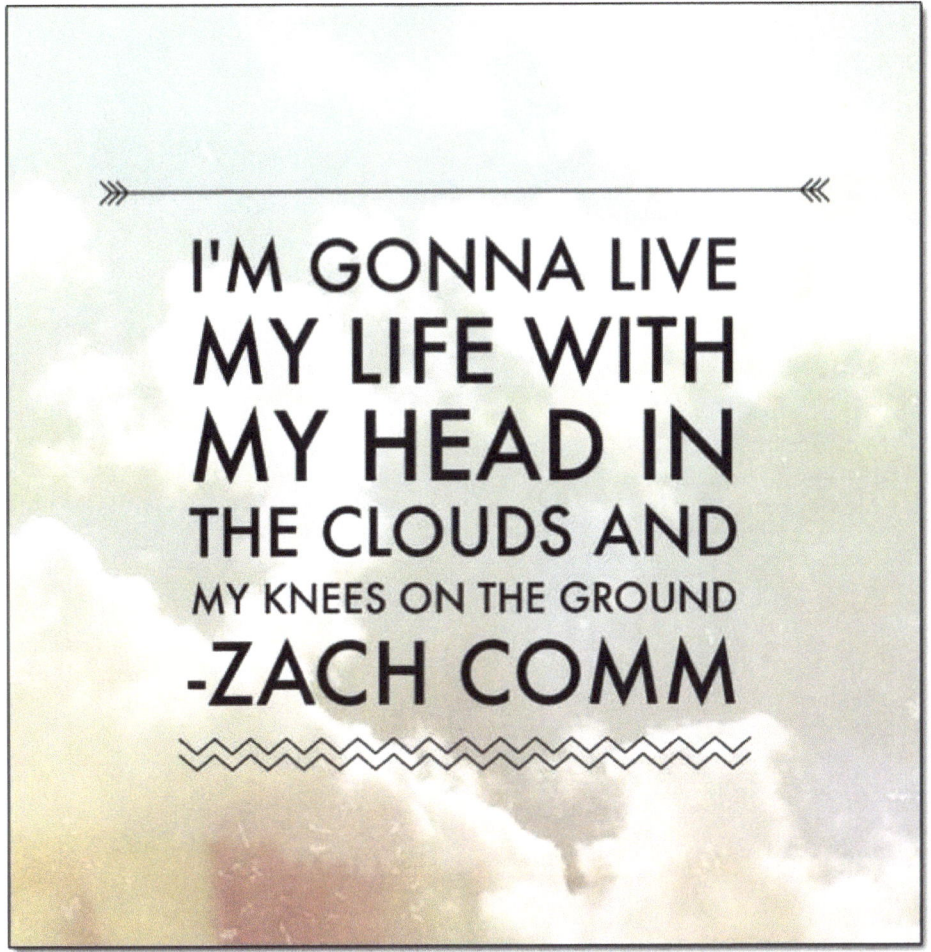

I'M GONNA LIVE MY LIFE WITH MY HEAD IN THE CLOUDS AND MY KNEES ON THE GROUND -ZACH COMM

I love my children. Without a doubt, raising two intelligent, thoughtful, funny, witty and kind-hearted children is an accomplishment that trumps everything else I have ever done. Sometimes one of them will say something remarkable. I saw my son, Zach, post these words and I knew I had to turn it into a photoquote. He is a dreamer and a young man of great faith. He understands the power of humility and prayer. This shout-out is for him and the lives that he will touch in the years to come.

IN MY QUEST TO NOT BE LIKE EVERYONE ELSE, *I'm going to* **LEARN HOW** *to put* **MY PANTS ON TWO LEGS AT** *a time*

— Joel Comm —

I saw this photo and thought I was taking a superhero stance. Recognizing I'm not a superhero, I thought it appropriate to come up with this bit of silliness. I'm just not afraid to be me.

We don't know how many days we have on this earth. Seize every one of them and seek to live your life to the fullest.

Music is the soundtrack of our lives. Wild Cherry nails it with these lyrics.

It's nice to have SOME lettuce
-BRIAN G JOHNSON

Here's my friend, Brian G. Johnson, fellow author also published by Morgan James Publishing. We were sharing a meal with several others when our food arrived. Brian noticed there was lettuce on his salad or burger, whatever it was. Then he profoundly stated that "it's nice to have some lettuce." Pure wisdom.

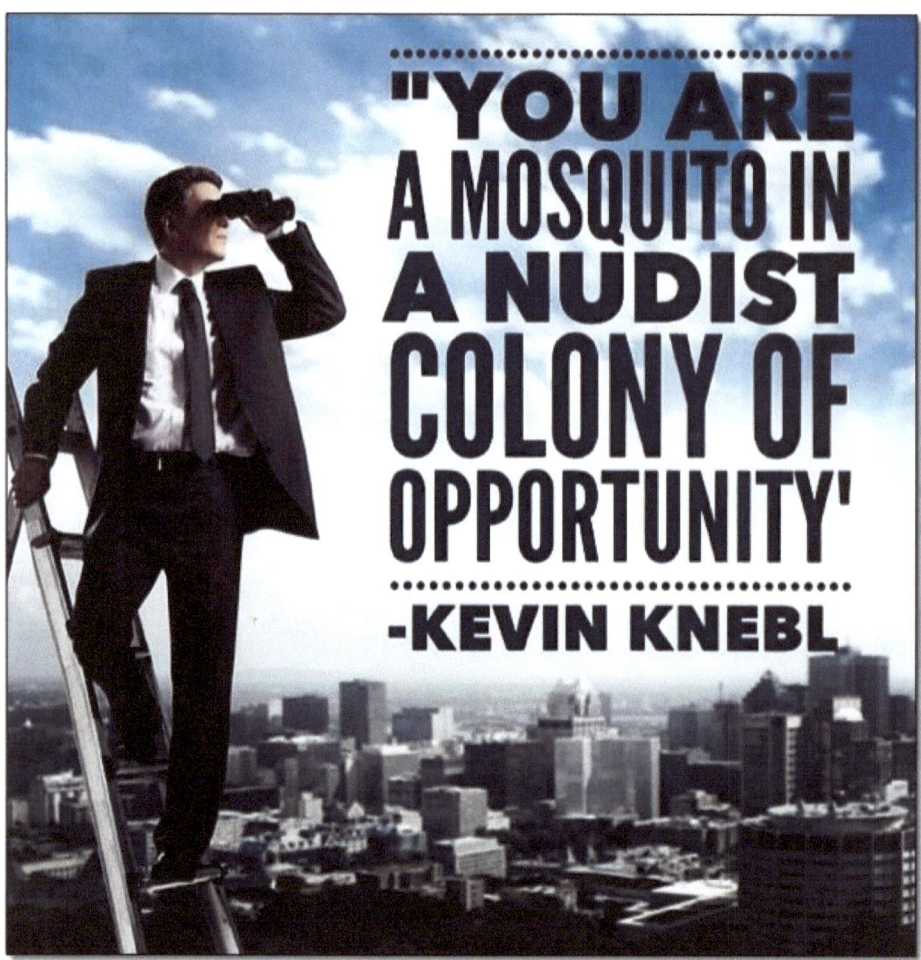

"YOU ARE A MOSQUITO IN A NUDIST COLONY OF OPPORTUNITY'
-KEVIN KNEBL

Kevin Knebl is a friend of mine who lives in Colorado. As we sat talking during a private meal, he shared this thought related to my career. I stopped and had to write it down because it was so good. I've got a lot of people I can recommend that you follow in the social space. @kevinknebl is one of them.

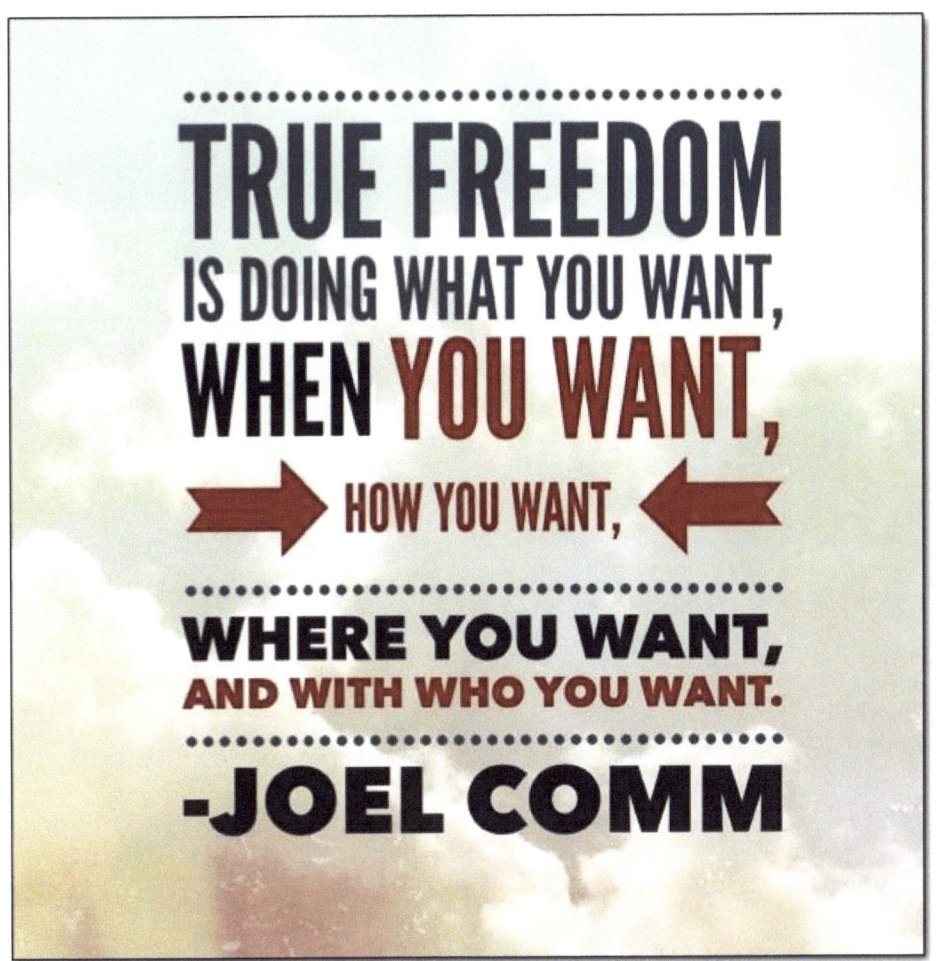

Many people have been sold a bill of goods as to what happiness is. I don't believe it is having a lot of money or acquiring more stuff. For me, having the freedom to do what I want with the people I like is a key to happiness.

YOU DON'T HAVE **TO SPEND** *another* DAY LIVING FOR **THE APPROVAL** OF OTHER **PEOPLE** ...

#joelsays

I know I'm not going to win over everyone. There will be some who just don't like me, for whatever reason. I'm fine with that and have decided it is more about them than me. I live for the approval of my God. If He is pleased with me, I don't have to worry about whether or not others approve of my choices.

There are some days when I just can't stop working. I guess that's because it doesn't feel like work. On this particular day I think I accomplished an entire weeks' worth of work in one day. It felt good.

Is It Magic?

People see my photoquotes and wonder if I am good at Photoshop or some other graphic design program. The truth is I am not really all that great at graphic design. However, I have found an iOS app that allows me to make photoquotes professionally and easily.

The app is called Wordswag, and it is available on the iTunes appstore.

And while I don't use any Android devices, there is a similar app for that platform called PicLab. You should be able to find it in the Google Play store.

Want more original social poetry?

Use the link below and go to SocialPoetryBook.com and register free to get access to the latest!

http://socialpoetrybook.com/

As for this ebook, it was put together using Brian G. Johnson's Magic Bullet Books and Kindle Ritual program which make formatting a breeze. Use the link below to learn more.

http://2014.kritual.com

About Joel Comm

Joel is a New York Times Best-Selling author of more than ten books with a dozen foreign translations and over 40 digital books in his catalog. As a pioneer of the World Wide Web, Joel has been creating profitable Internet businesses since 1995. Among his accomplishments are selling a site to Yahoo!, creating a #1 best-selling iPhone application, hosting and producing the world's first competitive Internet reality show, and being an in-demand International speaker. Currently a leader in the social media space, Joel's expertise is communicated via his blog, podcast, training materials and live events.

To connect with Joel on social media, visit him at:

http://facebook.com/joelcomm

http://twitter.com/joelcomm

http://linkedin.com/in/joelcomm

http://plus.google.com/joelcomm1

http://instagram.com/joelcomm

or go directly to the source and visit Joel's blog at http://www.JoelComm.com

More Books from Joel Comm

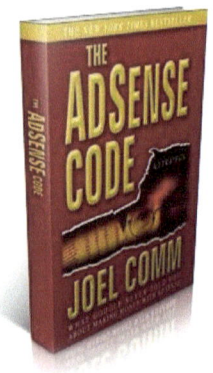

www.ingramcontent.com/pod-product-compliance
Lightning Source LLC
Chambersburg PA
CBHW040908180526
45159CB00010BA/2970